Copyright 2016, Doug Giles, All Rights Reserved

No part of this book may be reproduced, stored in a retrieval system, or transmitted by any means without the written permission of the author.

Illustrations and cover art by Doug Giles

Published by White Feather Press. (www.whitefeatherpress.com)

ISBN 978-1-61808-150-6

Printed in the United States of America

White Feather Press

Reaffirming Faith in God, Family and Country

A Coloring Book for College Cry Babies

by
Doug Giles

Introduction

Poor little Liberal college snowflakes are sad and dejected because Hillary didn't get elected. I, too, was once like you ... woebegone and forlorn. It was way back in 2012 when Obama got re-elected by you, sweet dandies. Herein, however, is where we differ.

When Obama was re-elected

1. I didn't vandalize my hometown.
2. I didn't pull my pants down in public and crap on a picture of Obama.
3. I didn't skip class, or my midterms, or go to a 'Primal Scream' meeting to have a good cry in a safe space.

No, instead, precious snowflakes, I went to work.

'What's work?' you ask.

Well, sweet snowflakes, it's where you provide goods, services and/or merchandise for others and they give you their money in exchange. You should google it between your masturbation sessions. It is quite amazing.

Yes, four years ago, when I was crestfallen and doleful over Obama beating Romney, I didn't roam the streets with other sad snowflakes looking for Don Lemon's camera to shout invectives into.

Indeed, instead of staying pouty, I built a massive news site called ClashDaily.com and we have since won many trophies for our hard work.

What's that you say, delicate snowflakes? You have never won a trophy? And the only award you have been given was a Participation Trophy? That's sad and unfair, gentle snowflakes.

I think you should be awarded a trophy because you do excel at one thing.

Yes, pouty snowflakes, you deserve an award.

My website ClashDaily.com would like to award you, fair snowflakes, with the 'Pussy Of The Year Award'! No one, and I mean no one has shown themselves more of a whiny, little squealy-ass pussy than you. Take pride. You're the best there is at being a pussy.

Oh, one more thing. In the event that you wish to stop being the Queen of Little Bitch Mountain, I wrote the perfect book for you.

It's called, PUSSIFICATION: The Effeminization of The American Male

That book, however, might be too rough for you, the mealy millennial. So, for now, content yourselves with and enjoy this coloring book I crafted just for you.

Doug Giles

Dear College Student:

Here's a coloring book just for you! We know you're angry that Trump got elected so we're here to help exorcise your devils and give you some much needed relief through coloring. If you haven't ever colored before, here are some tips to help you draw a pretty picture that you can cherish for years to come. It's pretty simple. Just try to stay inside the lines. That's it. Have fun and use all your crayons. Make your mommy and daddy proud. Hell, who knows ... they might even put it on their refrigerator for all your friends and relatives to see! God bless you, little Tinkerpot.

Your Friend,

Doug Giles

I know you're sad so here's a kitty to make you feel better! But please note: He's an angry cat who's ready to burn crap down, just like you!

Don't let the rich irony that most of you whiny bastards didn't even bother to vote annoy you because Hillary should've won regardless of voting. She deserves it because she has a vagina.

Being a pain in the ass really makes America love you. So, keep blocking traffic. But don't try that in Texas because they have big trucks and they'll run your ass over!

Before we proceed go to Starbucks and order a Venti Frappuccino and drink from that long green straw just like the little bitch that you are.

Don't let it bother you that you dudes supported a crooked old political chick who should be in prison and not our highest office in the land. Matter of fact, find another despicable candidate for 2020. Yahoo!

The State is my shepherd, I shall not want.
It makes me lie down in federally owned pastures.
It leads me beside quiet waters in banned fishing areas.
It restores my soul through its control.
It guides me in the path of dependency for its namesake.
Even though our nation plunges into the valley of the shadow of debt, I will fear no evil; for The State will be with me.
The Affordable Care Act and food stamps, they comfort me.
You prepare a table of Michelle Obama-approved foods before me in the presence of my Conservative and Libertarian enemies.
You anoint my head with hemp oil; my government-regulated, 16-ounce cup overflows.
Surely mediocrity and an entitlement mentality will follow me all the days of my life, and I will dwell in a low-rent HUD home forever and ever.

Amen.

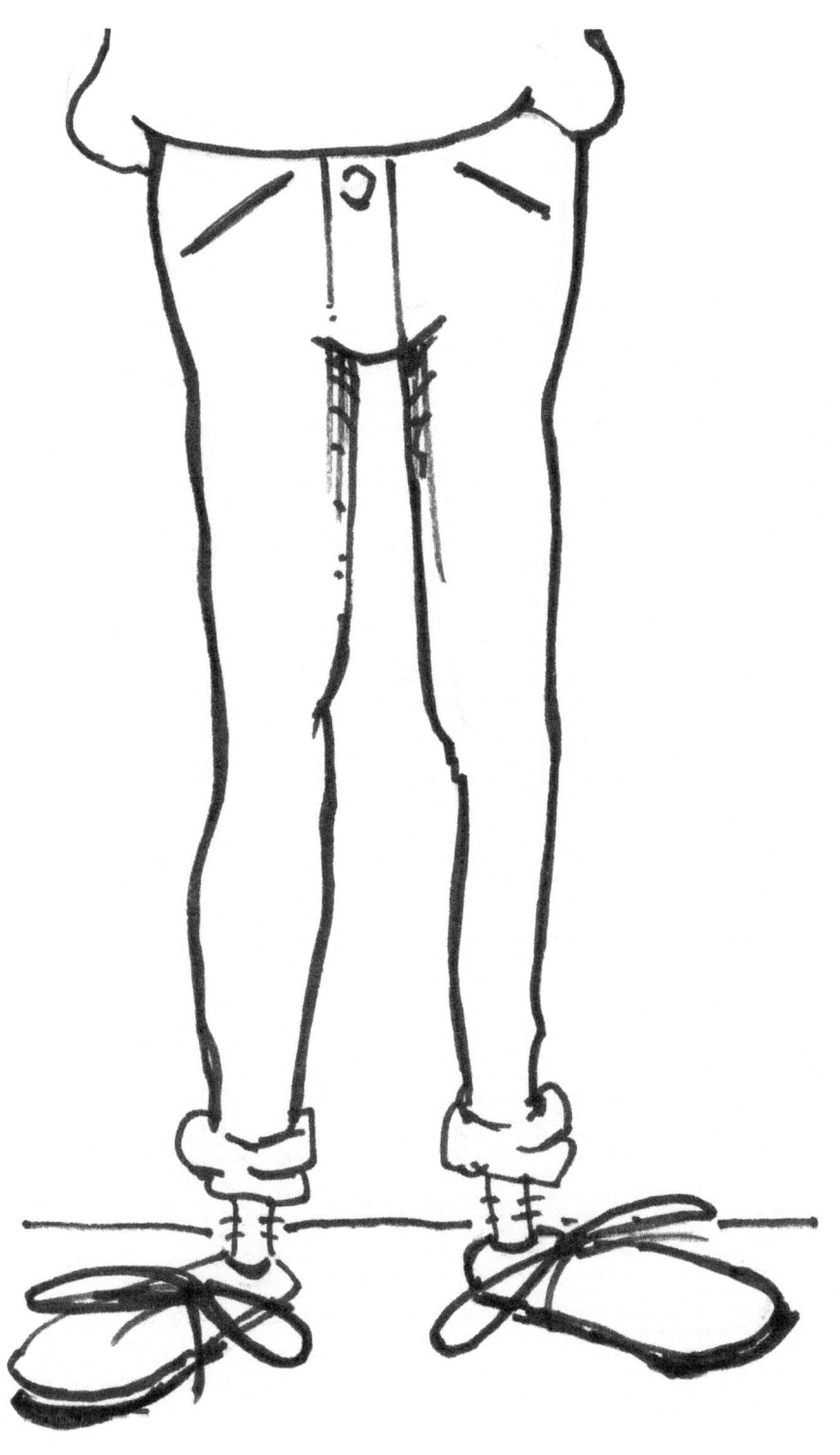

If you're still feeling blue and need a quick pick-me-up, go to the mall and get another pair of skinny jeans, you little pussy!

Also, we all know you loathe our country's Constitution so we drafted a more suitable document for you. Do you like it, or what? The Constitution of The United States of Pussification.

The Constitution of the United States of Pussification

We the Pussies of these sassy States,
In order to form a more fussy Union,
Establish Justin Bieber,
Insure domestic timidity,
Provide for a compromised defense,
Promote a continual Welfare State,

And secure diminishing Liberty for ourselves and our Posterity, do ordain and establish this Constitution for the United States of Pussification.

Article I – All cultural powers herein granted shall be vested in the most offended amongst us which shall consist of a Senate, whatever that is, and a House of Representatives made up of the man-hating ladies of *The View*.

Article II – The executive power shall be vested in a President of the United States of Pussification. He shall hold his Office as long as he doesn't become a Miss-All-That and a bag of potato chips, and, together with the Vice President, chosen primarily because he's cute and he's not afraid to go postal on Twitter, shall herein govern our fabulous collective.

Article III – The judicial power of the United States shall be vested in one Supreme Court, comprised of The E! Channel's Fashion Police and Kanye West, and in such inferior Courts as Kanye may from time to time ordain and establish according to his penchants. The judges, both of the supreme and inferior Courts, shall hold their Offices as long as they never listen to that asshat, Doug Giles.

Article IV – Full Faith and Credit shall be given in each State to the National Endowment of the Arts, EMI Records, and the more trendy Proceedings of every other State. And the Congress may by general Laws and stuff prescribe the Manner in which such thingies shall be proved, and the Effect thereof.

Article V – The Congress, whenever two thirds of both Houses think it's like important and all, shall propose Amendments to this Constitution, just as long as it doesn't ruin everything that we created.

Article VI – All Debts contracted and Engagements entered into, before the Adoption of this Constitution, shall not be valid against the United States of Pussification because that hurts our fragile Constitution, and should be deemed judgmental and not applicable because it's just so gross.

Article VII – The Ratification of the Conventions of these various States of Pussification shall be good enough for the Establishment of this Constitution between the States so ratifying the Same. So ... Enjoy.

Since you hate Trump so much and didn't get your way this election, you should load up the little amount of crap that you have and move to Canada.

Before we go on, take another break and get a sipple from your 50-year-old helicopter mommy's nipple.

Here's another poem for you. Roses are red. Violets are blue. And you're a pussy!

Because you love hash-tagging so much, here's a hashtag for you to color any way you wish. BTW, why are all the hashtags black? Uh ... hello! Racism!

When things don't go your way in life all classes and tests should be cancelled to suit your petulant demands because you're a Millennial.

Be offended and 'triggered' by anything and everyone. Sure people will hate you but that's okay. Your generation is the only one that matters!

It's time for a Play-Doh break, you little pussy!

If the Play-Doh didn't relieve your stress ... maybe this unicorn will. Please note: it's an angry unicorn just like you.

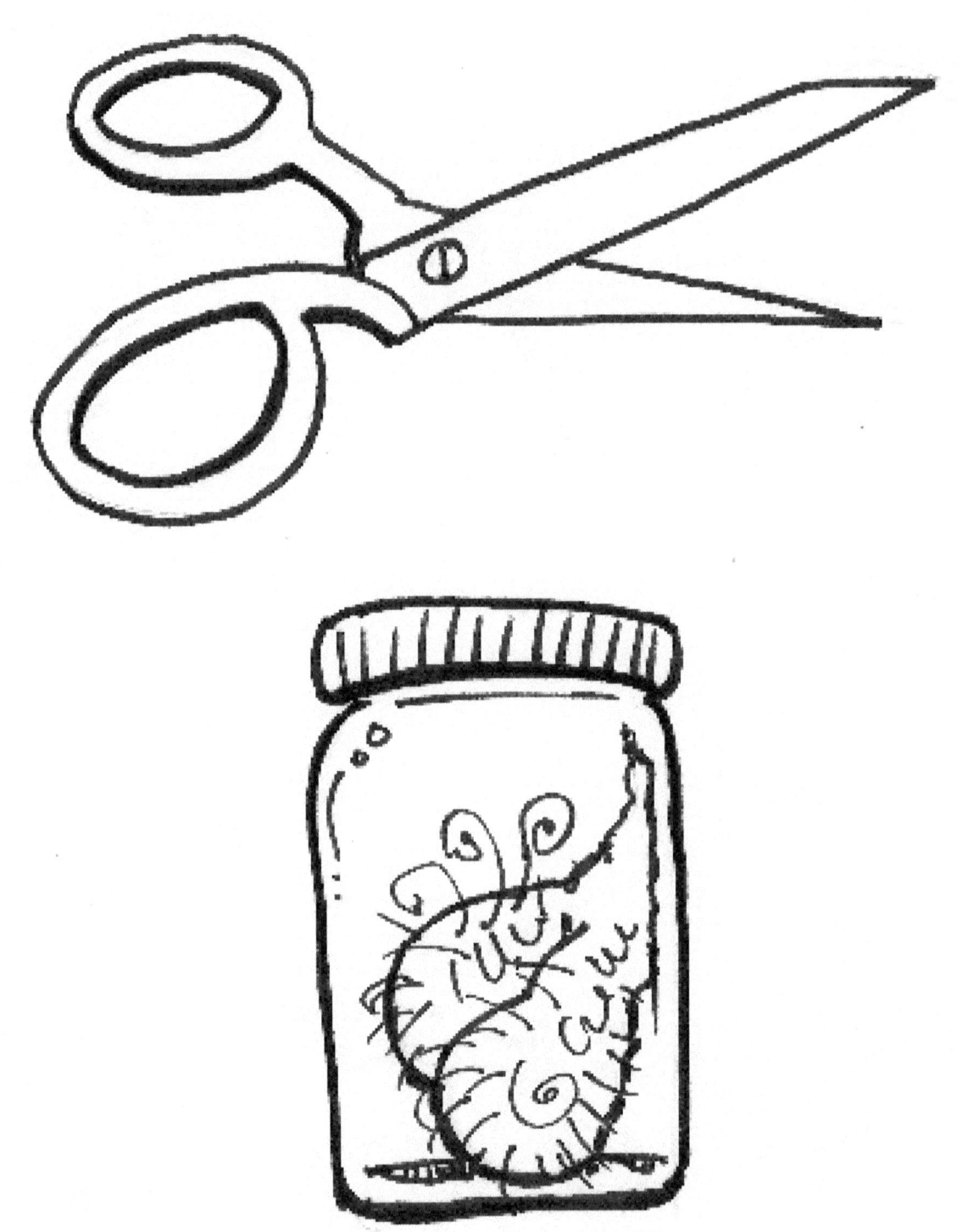

To expedite and make permanent your rank state of pussification, grab a pair of scissors and cut your balls off and put them in this jar!

Oh, my! Here's a picture of Sean Hannity! Make certain you put Devil's horns on him because he really ruined your world this last election.

Never let anyone shame you away from acting like a damn baby.

This is an Unemployment Check. It's what the government will send you after you graduate with your worthless degree in 'White Micro-Aggression Theory.'

If this coloring book hasn't helped you and you're still in despair ... then call The Wambulance to come pick your crippled ass up and take you to the 'I'm An Over-Coddled Pussy Clinic.'

More than likely you won't be able to find a job after graduating. Never fear! Selfies are here! Just take a ton of photos of your ass and up load 'em to Instagram.
Cha-Ching!

Finally, we give you a pic of President Donald J. Trump to color. Try to stay in the lines. I know you're angry but try to control your coloring and shading. Oh, and by the way, he just might turn our economy around and help you get a job. So, always stand ready to forgive if he succeeds where the Big Government goons have truly let you miserably down.

About the Author

Doug Giles is the man behind ClashDaily.com. In addition to driving ClashDaily.com, Giles is the author of eight books including his best-seller, *Raising Righteous and Rowdy Girls*.

Doug's articles have also appeared on several other print and online news sources, including *Townhall.com*, *The Washington Times*, *The Daily Caller*, *Fox Nation*, *USA Today*, *The Wall Street Journal*, *The Washington Examiner*, *American Hunter* magazine and *ABC News*.

Giles and his wife Margaret have two daughters: Hannah, who devastated ACORN with her 2009 nation-shaking undercover videos, and Regis who is a huntress, and owner of GirlsJustWannaHaveGuns.com

DG's interests include guns, big game hunting, big game fishing, fine art, cigars, helping wounded warriors, and being a big pain in the butt to people who dislike God and the USA.

Accolades for Giles and ClashDaily.com include …

– Giles was recognized as one of "The 50 Best Conservative Columnists of 2015"

– Giles was recognized as one of "The 50 Best Conservative Columnists of 2014"

– Giles was recognized as one of "The 50 Best Conservative Columnists of 2013"

– ClashDaily.com was recognized as one of "The 100 Most Popular Conservative Websites For 2013"

– Doug was noted as "Hot Conservative New Media Superman" By Politichicks

Speaking Engagements.

Doug Giles speaks to college, business, community, church, advocacy and men's groups throughout the United States and internationally. His expertise includes issues of Christianity and culture, masculinity vs. metrosexuality, big game hunting and fishing, raising righteous kids in a rank culture, the Second Amendment, personal empowerment, politics, and social change. For availability, please contact us at clash@clashdaily.com. Please use 'SPEAKING ENGAGEMENT' for your subject line when sending your request.

Other books by Doug Giles

PUSSIFICATION: The Effeminization of The American Male

Raising Righteous and Rowdy Girls

Raising Boys Feminists Will Hate

Ruling in Babylon: Seven Habits of Highly Effective Twentysomethings

Political Twerps, Cultural Jerks, Church Quirks

The Bulldog Attitude: Get It or Get Left Behind

10 Habits of Decidedly Defective People: The Successful Loser's Guide to Life

A Time to Clash: Papers from a Provocative Pastor

If You're Going Through Hell Keep on Going

Coming the fall of 2017

Hunting and The Bible: Is God Against Putting The Bam To Bambi?

PUSS-I-FI-CA-TION: The act, or process, of a man being shamed, taught, lead, pastored, drugged or otherwise coerced or cajoled into throwing out his brain, handing over his balls and formally abandoning the rarefied air of the testosterone-leader-fog that God and nature hardwired him to dwell in, and instead become a weak, effeminate, mangina sporting, shriveled up little pussy. * From The Doug Giles 2016 Dictionary of Grow the Hell Up, You Pussy!   In Giles' latest, and most raucous book, he takes 'Generation Pussy' from the warm wet womb of 'Pussville' to the rarefied air of 'Mantown.' This is definitely one of the most politically incorrect books to ever hit the market. It will most certainly offend the entitled whiners, but it will also be a breath of fresh air to young males who wish to be men versus hipster dandies.

Available at Amazon.com

It has been said that daughters are God's revenge on fathers for the kind of men they were when they were young. Some would say that both Doug Giles and I, given our infamous pasts, are charter members of that club. However, Doug and I know that his two wonderful daughters and my equally wonderful daughter and two granddaughters are truly God's fantastic gift. With the wisdom of hindsight and experience Doug has written the ultimate manual for dads on raising righteous and rowdy daughters who will go out into the world well prepared- morally, physically, intellectually and with joyful hearts- to be indomitable and mighty lionesses in our cultural jungle. Through every raucous and no-holds-barred page, Doug, the incomparable Dad Drill Sergeant, puts mere men through the paces to join the ranks of the few, the proud, and the successful fathers of super daughters. The proof of Doug Giles' gold-plated credentials are Hannah and Regis Giles- two of the most fantastic, great hearted and accomplished young ladies I have ever known. This is THE BOOK that I will be giving the father of my two precious five and three year old granddaughters. Tiger Mom meet Lion Dad!

— Pat Caddell

Fox News Contributor —

www.ingramcontent.com/pod-product-compliance
Lightning Source LLC
Chambersburg PA
CBHW001331010126
42453CB00013B/2382